Explore!
CIRCUSES

Liz Gogerly

Published in 2015 by Wayland

Copyright © Wayland 2015

Wayland
338 Euston Road
London NW1 3BH

Wayland Australia
Level 17/207 Kent Street
Sydney, NSW 2000

Editors: Victoria Brooker and Julia Adams
Designer: Elaine Wilkinson
Picture Researcher: Shelley Noronha
Illustrations for step-by-steps: Peter Bull

British Library Cataloguing in Publication Data

Circuses. -- (Explore!)
1. Circus--Juvenile literature.
I. Series
791.3-dc23

First published in 2012 by Wayland

ISBN 978 0 7502 8395 3

Printed in China

Wayland is a division of Hachette Children's
Books, an Hachette UK company

www.hachette.co.uk

Picture acknowledgements:
The author and publisher would like to thank the
following agencies and people for allowing these
pictures to be reproduced:

Cover (top LH image) & p. 5 (top): Corbis; p. 4:
Historical Picture Archive/Corbis; p. 5 (bottom)
Marilyn Kingwill/ArenaPAL; p. 6: The Art Archive/
Museo Nazionale Terme Rome/Gianni Dagli Orti;
pp. 6/7: LLC/Corbis; p. 7 (top): Bertrand Guay/
AFP/Getty Images; p. 8: The Granger Collection/
TopFoto; p. 9 (top): Wikimedia Commons; p. 9
(bottom): Everett Collection/Rex Features; p. 11
(top): Bill McCay/WireImage/Getty Images;
p. 11 (bottom): The Granger Collection/TopFoto;
p. 12: Walter Lockwood/Getty Images; p. 13
(top): Photoshot/Deborah Law; p. 13 (bottom)
& p. 31 (top): Giffords Circus; p. 14: Photoshot/
Band Photo; p. 15 (bottom): ZUMA Wire Service/
Alamy; p. 16: NBCU Photo Bank via Getty
Images; p. 17: Vincent de Vries photography/
Alamy; p. 20: Yuri Kochetkov/epa/Corbis; pp.
20/21: LukeMacGregor/Reuters/Corbis; p. 24:
Mike Stone/Alamy; p. 25 (top): Getty; p. 25
(bottom): Photoshot/Agencia el Universal; p.
26: AFP PHOTO/Stan HONDA; p. 27: Rowena
Chowdrey/TopFotoAll other images and creative
graphics: Shutterstock

Contents

The circus is in town!

The circus is one of the most popular forms of entertainment in the world. From China and Russia to the USA and Australia, people have been enjoying circus performances for decades, even centuries.

Philip Astley's circus entertained crowds in London in the late-1700s.

The beginning

In Ancient Rome, 'circus' was the name for a huge arena with seating around a U-shaped performance space. People would gather in a circus to watch spectacles such as chariot racing, beast hunts and plays.

The first circus to look like the circuses we know today was started in London in 1768 by Philip Astley. In 1782, another English man called Charles Dibdin became the first person to call his show a circus. In 1793, John Bill Ricketts took his English circus to America.

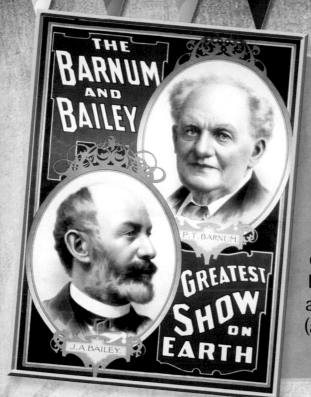

A poster advertising the Barnum & Bailey Circus in the 1800s.

Circuses in the USA

As soon as it was introduced in the USA, the circus became very popular, and buildings for circuses were erected in major cities. After the invention of the circus tent in 1825, circuses were able to travel, and more people were able to enjoy their performances. One of the most famous circuses during that time was the American circus Barnum & Bailey. They travelled the country in a train, and performed in a tent that had two (and later, up to seven) rings and stages.

Modern circus

In the 1960s, contemporary circus was born. Some performers wanted to create shows that combined circus, theatre, music and dance. They wanted to keep circus skills alive but tell a story at the same time. The French circus called Archaos is often called the first contemporary circus. The Canadian Cirque du Soleil is possibly now the best-known contemporary circus in the world. It was founded in 1984 by a group of street performers, and is still touring around the world today.

Cirque du Soleil has stunned audiences around the world since the 1980s.

The first circuses

The word circus comes from the Latin word for 'circle' or 'ring'. Latin was the language of the Ancient Romans who built the first circuses.

Horses and other animals were part of the entertainment at the Circus Maximus.

Circus Maximus

The Circus Maximus was a large stadium built in a valley in Rome in about sixth century BCE. The stadium could pack in 250,000 spectators, who came to watch the chariot races or marvel at the acrobats, jugglers, wild animals and gladiator fights. Although it wasn't like the circus performances we know today, an event in the Circus Maximus did bring people from all backgrounds together. Entrance was free and at the time, it was the only performance space where women and men were allowed to sit together.

Travelling performers

Fairs were an important part of life throughout Europe, especially after the Roman Empire declined in the fifth century CE. Many fairs were held during religious festivals and customers enjoyed the entertainment on offer. Traveller people, such as the Roma, performed acrobatics, juggled and danced with their trained animals. Many of these acts later became part of traditional circus shows.

The three generations of the French circus family Gruss. Their shows include many of the traditional acts that traveller people, such as the Roma, first performed.

Father of the modern circus

The first circus to look and feel like the traditional circus of today was started by Philip Astley in 1768 in London, England. This earned Astley the nickname 'father of the modern circus'. The ex-army man was an excellent horse trainer and regularly entertained the crowds with his bareback riding and horse tricks. In the 1760s, he opened a riding school in London and put on shows that proved very popular. In 1770, he decided to add more acts to the bill, including clowns, ropewalkers, acrobats, a pig that could do sums and a strong man called Hercules. He named it 'Astley's Amphitheatre'.

Adverts for Astley's circuses showed the energy of the entertainment.

Travelling circuses

When John Bill Ricketts came to the USA in 1793, he set up the first circus ring in the country in Philadelphia. It wasn't long before many other circuses were set up in large American cities.

THE BARNUM & BAILEY GREATEST SHOW ON EARTH

WONDERFUL PERFORMING GEESE, ROOSTERS AND MUSICAL DONKEY.

America's travelling shows

In the 1800s, settlers in the USA were moving westwards and setting up farms and homesteads. However, these people did not have easy access to large cities, so for a while, only a limited amount of people were able to enjoy circus entertainment.

In 1825, circus owner Joshuah Purdy Brown had the simple idea of using a canvas tent for performances. This made circuses quicker and easier to set up and it was now also possible to perform to people in remote areas. The idea caught on. By 1840, circuses in England began touring with tents, too.

Travelling circuses brought spectacular shows to many parts of the UK and USA.

English touring circus

The early touring circuses in England were small and often run by one family. Pablo Fanque owned one of the most successful travelling circuses in Victorian Britain. Pablo was a talented horseman and rope dancer, but he is best remembered for being the only black circus owner in Britain. His travelling show hit the road in the 1840s and ran for over 30 years.

Circus owner Pablo Fanque.

GENERAL VIEW OF THE TWELVE COLOSSAL WATER PROOF CANVAS PAVILIONS, EXACTLY THE SAME AS WILL BE ERECTED, BENEATH WHICH TWO GRAND EXHIBITIONS ARE GIVEN EVERY WEEK DAY. THEY ARE THE LARGEST AND FINEST CANVAS PAVILIONS EVER ERECTED ANYWHERE ON EARTH.

THE WORLD'S LARGEST, GRANDEST, BEST AMUSEMENT INSTITUTION

Barnum & Bailey's train brought their circus to all corners of the USA.

The circus train

Circus history would not be complete without the American circus owners Phineas Taylor Barnum (1810–1891) and William Cameron Coup (1837–1895). Together, they ran the Barnum & Bailey circus. In 1872, Coup developed the idea of the circus train. From the spring of that year, the circus travelled the length and breadth of the country in 65 railroad cars. This meant that the circus could travel further and faster, sometimes travelling as far as 160 kilometres in a single night.

Traditional circuses today

To this day, the traditional circus remains popular all over the world. From the eighteenth century to the present, the elements that make a traditional circus performance have remained almost unchanged.

A Big Top has enough space for a large audience and high-flying acts!

The Big Top

Traditional circuses usually hold performances in their main tent, or Big Top. This tent has space to seat hundreds of audience members, and enough height to accommodate trapezes and high wires. It takes a large team of people to set up a Big Top. Some circuses use motors, but it can still take nearly a day to raise this main tent. The Cole Brothers Circus in America is one of the largest travelling circuses in the world today and has an enormous Big Top measuring 41.5 metres wide by 57 metres long. It can seat up to 2,300 people.

The ringmaster

At the start of most circus shows the ringleader, or ringmaster, enters the ring. They are in charge of the show and introduce the acts, usually in a loud booming voice. Traditionally, the ringmaster wears a top hat and tails – the brighter the better! It is their job to get the crowd excited before each act enters the ring. Sometimes, they have their own act or they play along with the clowns.

The ringmaster traditionally gets the show started.

Circus music

Traditional circus music involves plenty of drum-rolls and fast marches, and all the acts are choreographed to go with the music. In the past, circuses had their own band with drums, organ and brass instruments. Nowadays, most circuses use recorded music, so they no longer perform with a band. While traditional circuses still perform to marches and brass band music, contemporary circuses have taken the music they use in a new direction. Composers write music that adds atmosphere and helps to tell the story. You might also hear hip-hop and other kinds of popular music as the performers take to the stage.

Animals in the ring

In the past, animals were the stars of the show in many traditional circuses. Now that audiences are more aware of animal rights, you are more likely to see people, rather than animals, in the ring.

An elephant strikes a pose in a traditional circus act.

Trained to entertain

Wild animal circus acts began in the 1820s. Isaac A. Van Amburgh (1801–1865), a wild animal trainer, stunned American audiences when he put his arm inside a lion's mouth and his head between the jaws of a tiger. Since then, crowds have been entertained by all kinds of trained animals. Elephants, seals, monkeys, tigers and lions, as well as horses and dogs, have been taught to rise up on their back legs, leap through burning rings, and perform handstands and dances for people's entertainment. One of the most famous wild animals in the circus was Jumbo the elephant. He joined Barnum & Bailey Circus in 1881.

Animal rights activists protest against the cruel treatment of some circus animals.

Animal welfare

In the late-twentieth century, people began to question the use of animals in circuses. The average circus animal spends a lot of time travelling, which can be stressful. While on tour, they have to live in small enclosures or cages with little or no access to the outdoors. Animal cruelty is another big problem. Some circus animals can be whipped or hit during training.

Circus animals today

Animal welfare charities are working hard towards banning wild animals in circuses all around the world. At the moment, the only country that bans the use of animals in entertainment is Greece. However, many circuses no longer use animals in their acts, and instead focus their shows on acrobatics and stunts. Some circuses, such as Giffords Circus in the UK, still include animal acts in their performances. However, they say that they make sure the animals get treated well, are able to rest, and the horses spend part of the year in fields.

Horses, geese and even barn owls are part of the performance at Giffords Circus.

Circus performers

The bill for a circus changes each year, but no show is complete without some of the traditional acts. Most of these have been performed since the nineteenth century.

The trapeze is one of the most skilled aerial acts.

Up in the air

Aerial acts are a highlight of the circus. They involve acrobats performing stunts in the air – on the trapeze, hoops, swings or even bands of silk. It takes incredible strength, balance and skill to perform any aerial act, and acrobats train for years, often using safety nets to prevent accidents. The trapeze was invented by Jules Léotard from France in the mid-nineteenth century. He used to practise his trapeze act over a swimming pool. The all-in-one knitted suit he wore became known as the leotard.

Clowning around

It's the job of the clowns to bring fun and laughter to the circus ring. Every clown creates their own 'face' and character. It's an unwritten rule that clowns do not copy each other. The oldest kind of clown is called a whiteface clown. They wear all white and don't use much make-up. Auguste clowns became popular in America in the late-nineteenth century. They often wear big, baggy clothes, big shoes and a red nose. They use lots of face paint around their mouths and eyes.

Juggling

Jugglers have always been one of the main acts at the circus. This is a skilled performance that needs hours of practice every day. All kinds of props can be used including balls, bags, clubs, hoops, diabolos, hats, plates, swords and fire torches. Master jugglers can roll the props off different parts of their body or juggle with one hand. Nowadays, circus jugglers compete to create the most amazing routines. Anthony Gatto of the Cirque du Soleil is one of the most famous jugglers in the world and holds 12 world records for his juggling skills.

Auguste clowns are known for their big shoes, red noses and funny faces.

Anthony Gatto juggles a handful of rings while bouncing a ball on his head during rehearsals.

The show stoppers

There has always been tough competition between different circuses. Every circus wants to attract the biggest audience, so they have to offer amazing acts to draw in the crowds. Some of these acts even break world records!

Human cannonballs

The human cannonball is one of the most thrilling acts of many circuses. The person is ejected from the cannon by a jet of compressed air or a spring. The first human cannonball was a teenage girl called Rosa 'Zazel' Richter who stunned audiences in Victorian London as she was fired into the air and landed on a net. In 2011, David 'The Bullet' Smith Jr set a new world record for distance travelled by a human cannonball. He flew 59.05 metres at a speed of 110 kilometres per hour!

Human cannonball world-record holder David 'The Bullet' Smith Jr.

Stunts

Many circus acts not only include acrobatics and skills such as juggling and unicycling, but also jaw-dropping stunts. The most popular ones involve motorcyclists performing flips, jumps and spins at high speed. The Globe of Death is a stunt during which up to eight motorcyclists ride around in a metal globe, performing loops and other tricks. A similar stunt is the Wall of Death. Here, the performers ride around the vertical walls of a cylinder-shaped container. Both stunts are spectacular, but incredibly dangerous, and have often led to serious accidents.

Only highly-trained motorcyclists perform the Wall of Death.

Acts in flames

Many circus acts add a twist to traditional performances by using fire. Jugglers and acrobats add an element of danger by juggling torches, jumping through fire hoops and performing complex acrobatic routines with burning staffs, hoops and swords. In the past, circuses even trained animals, such as lions and tigers, to jump through flaming hoops. However, most circuses no longer include this as part of their act, as it can cause the animals great distress.

Fire-eating is another highly-skilled and dangerous circus act.

Learn to juggle

In the past people joined a circus and learned skills from the other performers. These days you don't need to runaway to the circus to learn a circus skill. Juggling is something you can practise at home or anywhere there is space. When you've mastered juggling three objects, try five. The world-record holders can juggle up to 13 objects, so go for it!

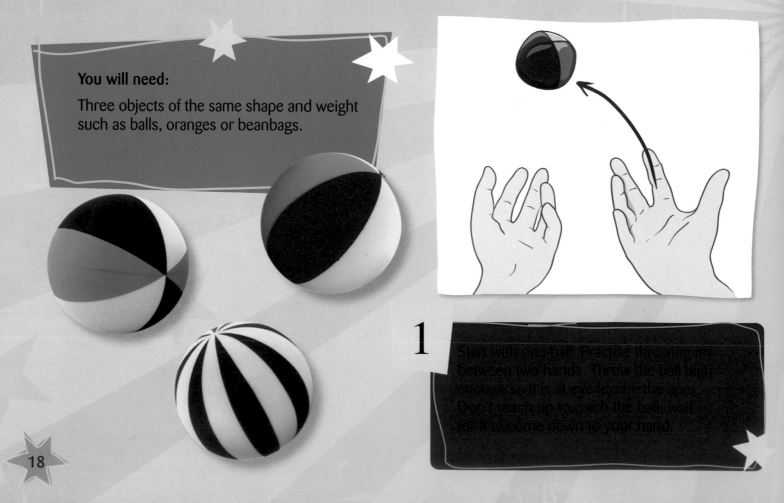

You will need:

Three objects of the same shape and weight such as balls, oranges or beanbags.

1

Start with one ball. Practise throwing it between two hands. Throw the ball high enough so it is at eye level – the apex. Don't reach up to catch the ball, wait for it to come down to your hand.

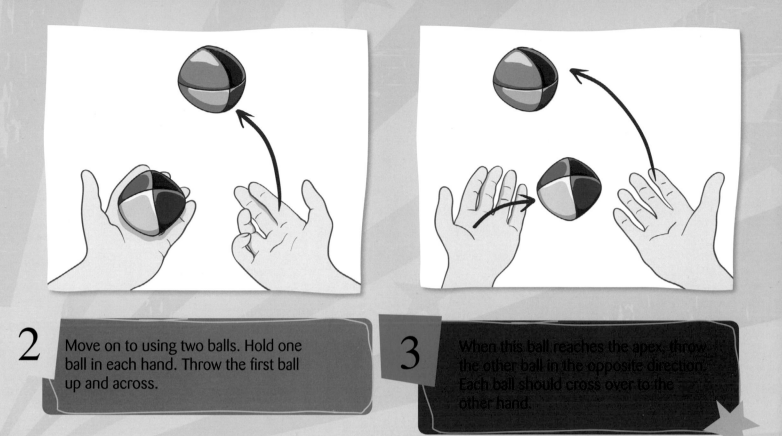

2 Move on to using two balls. Hold one ball in each hand. Throw the first ball up and across.

3 When this ball reaches the apex, throw the other ball in the opposite direction. Each ball should cross over to the other hand.

4 Once you can juggle two balls without thinking, you are ready for three balls! To begin, hold two balls in the hand you are going to start with and one in the other. The first two throws you make are the same as with two balls.

5 When the second ball is coming down, throw the third ball. If done correctly, all three balls should end up in the opposite hand from where they started. Repeat

When you get good at juggling balls, you can move on to rings, clubs or sticks.

The great state circuses

Some countries have a travelling state circus that tours regularly. Every national circus has its own style and many impressive acts. The Moscow State Circus and Chinese State Circus entertain huge crowds all around the world.

Performing elephants are one of the highlights of the Moscow State Circus.

Moscow State Circus

Russia is very proud of its circuses. People in Russia believe that the circus is an art form, just like ballet, theatre, classical music and opera. The country takes circus skills so seriously that state circus schools were opened throughout Russia in the 1920s. Students often trained up to 20 hours a day. The Moscow State Circus is famous for its skilled performers, as well as the traditional music, dancing and storytelling.

Great building

While part of the Moscow State Circus tours the world with its performances, many of the artists remain in Moscow and perform in a permanent building there. The building can seat up to 3,400 people and its main performance area is 36 metres high. The ring can be changed, so the crowd can enjoy water and ice acts, too.

Circus performers take to the stage in Moscow.

Shaolin Warriors perform a daring sword routine.

Chinese State Circus

The Chinese State Circus has been touring the world since the 1990s. Their shows are a dazzling display of Chinese culture that goes back thousands of years. The troupe wears traditional Chinese costume and dresses up as characters from folk stories and traditional tales. Music, dance and mime add to the storytelling. Many people love the death-defying displays of martial arts by the Shaolin Warriors. They break poles and concrete blocks across their bodies, and walk over swords.

Contemporary circuses

In recent years, circuses all over the world have broken away from the traditional style. They are known as contemporary circuses.

Circus Smirkus is a youth circus founded in Vermont, USA, in 1997. The troupe is aged between 10 and 18. Performers get involved in all aspects of the circus including selling tickets, working in the kitchens and helping backstage.

Lucent Dossier Experience is a cutting-edge circus from Los Angeles, USA. They perform aerial acts in birdcages and spider webs. Look out for the bearded lady and the snake charmer!

Circus Baobab from Guinea, West Africa, is a troupe of acrobats and percussionists. This circus mixes traditional and modern aspects of African culture in its storytelling.

The first contemporary circus

In 1986, a group of French performers formed a circus known as Archaos. This circus was more theatrical and imaginative than previous circuses. It was often called the 'punk' circus because the performers looked more like members of a punk band than traditional circus acts. Their amazing acts included chainsaw juggling and fire breathing.

Swedish circus **Cirkus Cirkör** formed in Stockholm in 1995. The acrobats, clowns and other circus acts combine music, dance, acting and film in their shows.

Circus Oz from Australia formed in Melbourne in 1978. These lively performers bring humour, modern rock music and stunning circus skills into the ring.

Life behind the scenes

A lot of hard work goes into making the circus an exciting event. People in the audience are focused on the glittering performances, but life behind the scenes is very different.

Costumes and props

In many circuses the performers do their own costume, hair and make-up. However, Cirque du Soleil employs over 300 people to create its dazzling costumes and make-up. Cirque has shows on all around the world. When a show reaches a new destination, the Head of Wardrobe employs local people, such as stitchers, craft technicians, dressers, wig dressers and laundry staff. The stitchers are on hand to mend costumes and replace buttons. The craft technicians do anything from gluing soles on shoes to painting masks.

A huge team are involved in the stunning costumes and make-up of the Cirque du Soleil performers.

All aboard!

A travelling circus spends much of the year working and living on the road. Many circus employees live in caravans or temporary accommodation. In America, the Ringling Brothers Circus has its own circus train. Over 250 employees of the circus, including the performers, animals, vets, mechanics, cooks and the train crew, live on the train. Some carriages, such as the 'Pie Car', are communal eating areas.

Circus trains even transport performing animals, such as elephants.

Life on the move

Touring and living together can be hard work. Robert Morgan tours the world with the Cirque du Soleil. He says it's not like an average job: "It's so diverse – it's diverse weather, it's diverse languages, it's diverse, you name it… We change a lot in Cirque as it is, so it's constant change." Some people cannot cope with the change, but Robert says that it's fascinating and exciting. He also says the rest of the circus becomes like a family: "You share everything together, so it's a wonderful experience."

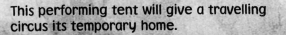
This performing tent will give a travelling circus its temporary home.

Circus careers

Running away to join the circus may sound like a dream. But it takes a lot of hard work and dedication to become a star in the Big Top. Meet some people who have made it into the ring...

Underwater circus star

Name: Brynn Butzman

Birthplace: Hamden, Connecticut, USA

Education: BS degree in Biology from Santa Clara University

Background: At 14, Brynn moved to California, USA, to pursue a career in synchronised swimming. She won the Junior Synchronised Swimming World Championships at 16 and was a finalist in the trials for the 2000 Olympics. Now, she is one of the synchronised swimmers in the Cirque du Soleil show 'O'.

Q Why did you join the Cirque du Soleil?

A Competing is great, but my favourite part was always performing in front of lots of people, getting to show off what I had worked so hard to accomplish. Cirque allows me to do that every night, twice a night.

Q What is the best part of the job?

A I love hearing the audience gasp during a big trick, laugh at a funny move, or enjoy the silence during a beautiful moment. Taking them out of the real world and bringing them into ours is a really special thing that very few people get to experience and be a part of.

The Cirque du Soleil show 'O' is performed regularly in Las Vegas. The entire show is performed in, on and around water.

Since 2006, NoFit State has been training its circus stars in Cardiff, Wales.

A real all-rounder

Howie Morley has been with the Welsh contemporary circus NoFit State for over 12 years. He's an all-rounder who can ride a unicycle, walk around on stilts and walk the tightrope. He was a farmer and never dreamed of being in the circus. That was until he went to see Archaos: "They had this great anarchic spirit. Crazy vehicles, lots of fire, beautiful trapeze artists. I thought, 'That looks fantastic! I really want to do that.'"

Howie spent ten years learning circus skills and in 1997, volunteered as a labourer for NoFit State. He didn't expect to perform but one day the director caught him walking on stilts and asked him to be part of the show. Howie reckons the circus isn't for everyone, but he loves the audience reaction to the show: "You are giving them something that is uplifting to the spirit… That's fantastic. You can't beat it."

Facts and figures

The Cirque du Soleil employs over 5,000 people around the world, including about 1,300 performers.

In 2003, Venezuelan Henry Ayala did 211 skips on a tightrope in one minute at Billy Smart's Circus in Bristol, UK. The wire was set 8.1 metres high.

Circus Krone, in Munich, Germany, is the largest circus in Europe. Its enormous tent can seat 5,000 people.

The Mexican Circo Atayde is the oldest touring circus in the world. It was founded in 1888 and has been run by the Atayde family ever since it started.

In June 2011, Russian circus artists Edgard Zapashny, Aleksandra Blinova and Kristina Gritsaenko set the record for the tallest human pillar on a moving horse. The trio stood on each others shoulders creating a human pillar that was 4.55 metres tall while the horse trotted around the ring.

In 1968, Ringling Brothers and Barnum & Bailey opened their Clown College. Two years later, in 1970, the first woman was accepted into the college.

German juggler Rudy Horn set the world record in 1951 by being the first person to catch six cups and saucers on top of his head while riding a tall unicycle! The objects landed in a stack balanced on his head. He was unable to see any of the catches.

Traditional circus bands play John Philip Sousa's 'Stars and Stripes Forever' if there is an emergency, such as a fire or an escaped animal. This lets all the circus staff know that something is seriously wrong.

The first quadruple back somersault to be performed on a flexible pole was achieved by Maxim Dobrovitsky of Russia on 4 February 1989.

Glossary

Acrobat Someone who performs... gymnastic...

Aerial act Circus act performed in the air on a trapeze or...

Amplitheatre A round or oval shaped building with rows of seats... live performances where audiences sit in seats in rows to look down at the arena.

Anarchic Without rules or laws...

Choreograph To arrange the order of the steps of a dance.

Compressed When something is much smaller than almost... is squeezed... to pay to ride in...

Debut A first...
an item or...
debut...
across the...

DJ Disc...

Glockenspiel A musical instrument that is played by striking metal bars...

Illusionist Someone who...
and moves... rather than...

Instrument An object...
rhythmic instrument such as a drum that is used to keep...

Orchestra A large group of musicians who... play...
instruments...

Further reading

BOOKS

Clowns of the 20th Century!: Photographs of 100 Years of Circus Clowns by David Jamieson (Aardvark Publishing, 2001)

101 Circus Games for Children by Paul Rooyackers (Hunter House Publishers, 2009)

The Great and Only Barnum: The Tremendous, Stupendous Life of Showman P.T. Barnum by Candace Fleming (Schwartz & Wade Books, 2009)

Who Was...? Philip Astley: The Inventor of the Circus by Nell Stroud (Short Books Ltd, 2003)

Websites

Chinese State Circus: www.chinesestatecircus.com

Circus Krone: www.circus-krone.de/en/index.html

Cirque du Soleil: www.cirquedusoleil.com

Moscow State Circus: www.moscowstatecircus.com

Ringling Brothers and Barnum & Bailey: www.ringling.com

The Victoria and Albert Museum's website, looking at the world of twentieth century circuses in the UK: www.vam.ac.uk/content/articles/0-9/modern-circus

A peep behind the scenes as the Culpepper & Merriweather Circus pulls into town: www.cmcircus.com/bts

The history of the circus by historian John Shepler: www.johnshepler.com/articles/circus.html

Index